The Wonder of You

by Harold Klemp

The Wonder of You
Copyright © 2014 ECKANKAR

All rights reserved. No part of this book may be reproduced, stored in a retrieval system, or transmitted in any form by any means, whether electronic, mechanical, photocopying, recording, or otherwise, without prior written permission of Eckankar.

The terms ECKANKAR, ECK, EK, MAHANTA, SOUL TRAVEL, and VAIRAGI, among others, are trademarks of ECKANKAR, PO Box 2000, Chanhassen, MN 55317-2000 USA. 180135

Printed in USA
Text from *The Call of Soul*, by Harold Klemp
Illustrated by April Munson
Edited by Patrick Carroll, Joan Klemp, and Anthony Moore
Second printing—2018

Library of Congress Cataloging-in-Publication Data

Klemp, Harold.
[Call of soul]
The wonder of you / by Harold Klemp.
pages cm
Rev. ed. of: The call of soul 2009.
Summary: "Author Harold Klemp, spiritual leader of ECKANKAR, illustrates for youth of all ages how to look for the blessings in life and see themselves as Soul"-- Provided by publisher.
ISBN 978-1-57043-395-5 (pbk. : alk. paper) 1. Eckankar (Organization) 2. Spiritual life--Eckankar (Organization) I. Title.
BP605.E3K5525 2014
299'.93--dc23
2014002793

∞ This paper meets the requirements of ANSI/NISO Z39.48-1992 (Permanence of Paper).

I0804301

Dedicated to you, a light of ECK

Who could be more wonderful than you?

You have, oh, so many blessings. All you need to do is recognize them.

Can you? Will you? Do you?

Look around.

You live in a garden.

Someone loved you so much that here you are,

in a garden.

There is spiritual food all around,
here to feed and nourish.
All you need to do is get it.

You are one of the special people. Somehow you've become awake and opened your eyes. Now awake, you know you are special.

You know you live in a very special garden, a garden of love.

Someone loved you so much
that you are here and awake.

What a blessing to know you are blessed.

So how'd you come to be?
How'd you get here?
Why?
And where to next?

Questions in the midst of plenty.
Thinking, thinking.
Why, why?

And, why, why?

All this and more is you,

a so-wonderful you.

Handmade in heaven.

Cared for on earth.

And all you have to do is accept it,

and you will recognize the wonder of you too.

Set your sights high. Set them very high. Why not set your sights on God?

God loves you and
has from Its creation of you.

You were handmade in heaven,
by the Maker of life, love, freedom,
and happiness.

Be happy, be you, just BE!

Put away your fear. Put away your doubt. And remember to put away your worry.

You are Soul. Special. One of a kind.

So love yourself, love God, and love others.

So look around and say thank you for all the blessings.

Wake up and sing!

Glory in this garden of love, because the holy foods are all around.

The best is yet to come.

Such is the wonder of you!

For Further Reading, Study, and Fun

When I Was Big

By Debbie Kaplan

Celebrate the child's imagination while opening the door to the possibility of past lives. Colorful illustrations explore a little boy's memories of being a hunter, voyager, king, nurse, teacher, farmer, sailor of the seas, and more.

Grandpa Went Away

By Debbie Kaplan

Explore what happens when a loved one—a relative, a pet, or a friend—passes on. A young boy finds that life's challenges and changes are all about divine love.

Davie Learns a Lesson about Karma

By Debbie Kaplan

The lesson Davie learns, that "Everything you do will come back to you," is just the beginning.
Find out what else Davie learns and what he does that earns him a gift that will last his whole life.

ECK Parable & Activity Kit for Youth

More than 300 fun, enriching activities you can use at home, at ECK Light and Sound Services, in ECK classes, and everywhere! Each illustrated parable, puzzle, and spiritual exercise leads your child to their own personal discoveries with the Mahanta. Ideal for ages three to thirteen.
You can find this kit at www.Eckankar.org in the Members Area under "Youth and Family Resources."

Gratitude Grab Bag and Other Ideas for ECK Youth Activities

Ideas for parents and teachers of ECK youth classes to teach youth about the Light and Sound of God.

Sounds of HU

By Crary Brouhard

A baby's cry, a lullaby, buzzing bees, the wind in the trees? How do ***you*** hear the HU?
No matter your age, this delightful, full-color children's picture book reminds us how the sound of HU is a divine gift that is heard and found in all life.

Available from Eckankar: www.Eckankar.org; (952) 380-2222; ECKANKAR, Dept. BK121, PO Box 2000, Chanhassen, MN 55317-2000 USA.

Illustrated ECK Parables

By Harold Klemp

Harold Klemp's parables have brought spiritual wisdom and inspiration to seekers everywhere. Available in beautiful, full-color booklets illustrated by artist Amanda Gunz, these parables will be treasured by youth of all ages.

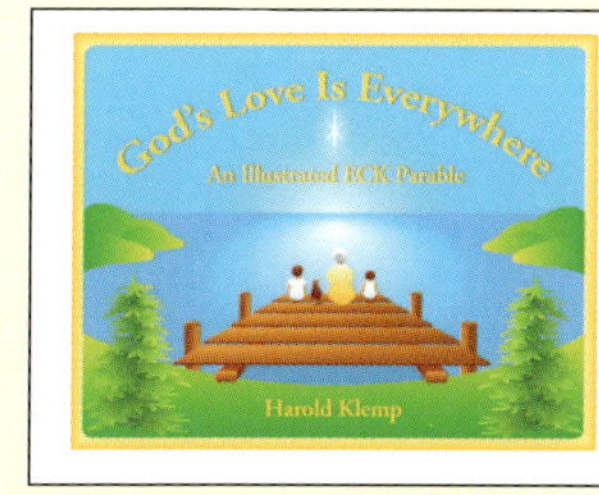

God's Love Is Everywhere

The Angry Camper

The Cat and the Hamsters

It Matters to This Starfish

The Bald Rooster

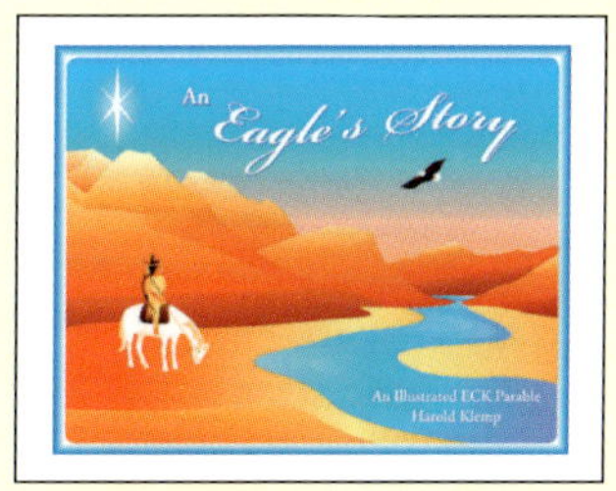

An Eagle's Story

Key of Opportunity

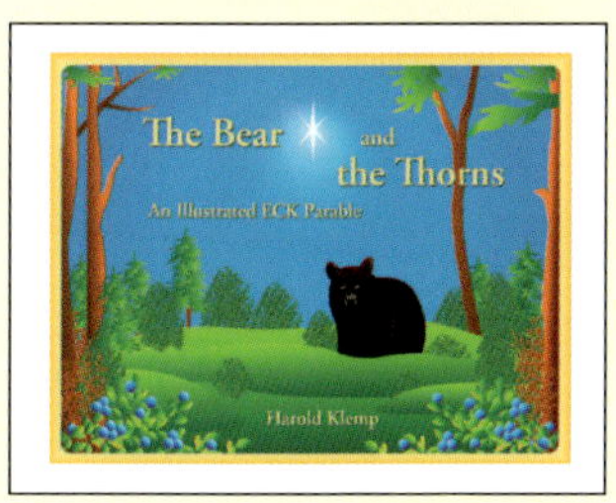

The Bear and the Thorns

Forest Family

Ladybug, Ladybug

Calf Paths of the Mind

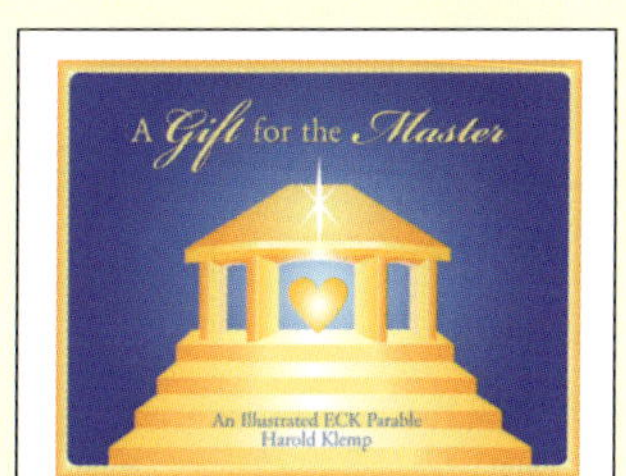

A Gift for the Master

Nubby and Sunshine

continued . . .

Available from Eckankar: www.Eckankar.org; (952) 380-2222; ECKANKAR, Dept. BK121, PO Box 2000, Chanhassen, MN 55317-2000 USA.

…More Illustrated ECK Parables

One Small Thing for Love

The Overcrowded House

Pappagena, Come Home!

The Peaceful Parrot

Peanut's Hard Road to Freedom

The Song That Makes God Happy

Sound of HU

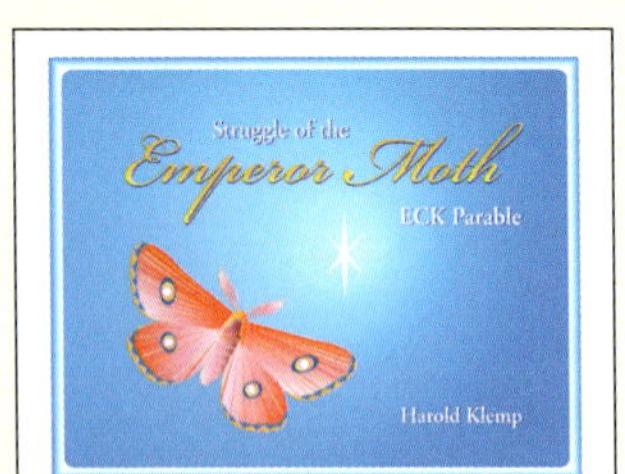

Struggle of the Emperor Moth

Illustrated ECK Parables on CD

Each CD contains a PowerPoint slide show of three illustrated parables for use in events for youth and families.

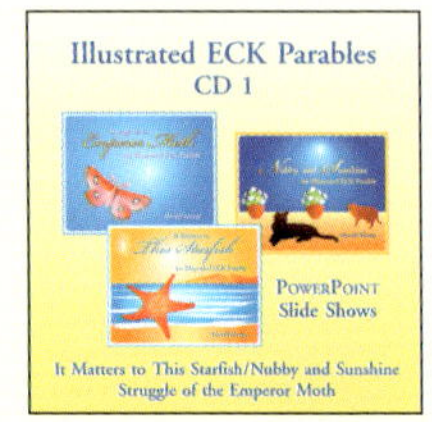

CD1: *It Matters to This Starfish; Nubby and Sunshine; Struggle of the Emperor Moth*

CD4: *The Cat and the Hamsters; Key of Opportunity; Ladybug, Ladybug*

CD2: *A Gift for the Master; One Small Thing for Love; The Song that Makes God Happy*

CD5: *The Angry Camper; Calf Paths of the Mind; The Overcrowded House*

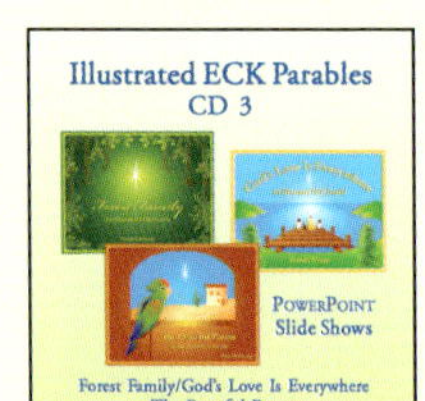

CD3: *Forest Family; God's Love Is Everywhere; The Peaceful Parrot*

CD6: *The Bald Rooster; The Bear and the Thorns; Pappagena, Come Home!*

CD7: *An Eagle's Story; Peanut's Hard Road to Freedom; Sound of HU*

CD8: *The Farmer and the Wood Duck; Giant Utensils of Heaven and Hell; The Japanese Gardener*

CD9: *Spiritual Lessons from "Harold and the Purple Crayon"; Golden Netting; The Nightingale's Song*

CD10: *The Reappearing Kittens; The Simplicity of Love; Walking the Dog*

Available from Eckankar: www.Eckankar.org; (952) 380-2222; ECKANKAR, Dept. BK121, PO Box 2000, Chanhassen, MN 55317-2000 USA.